I0821860

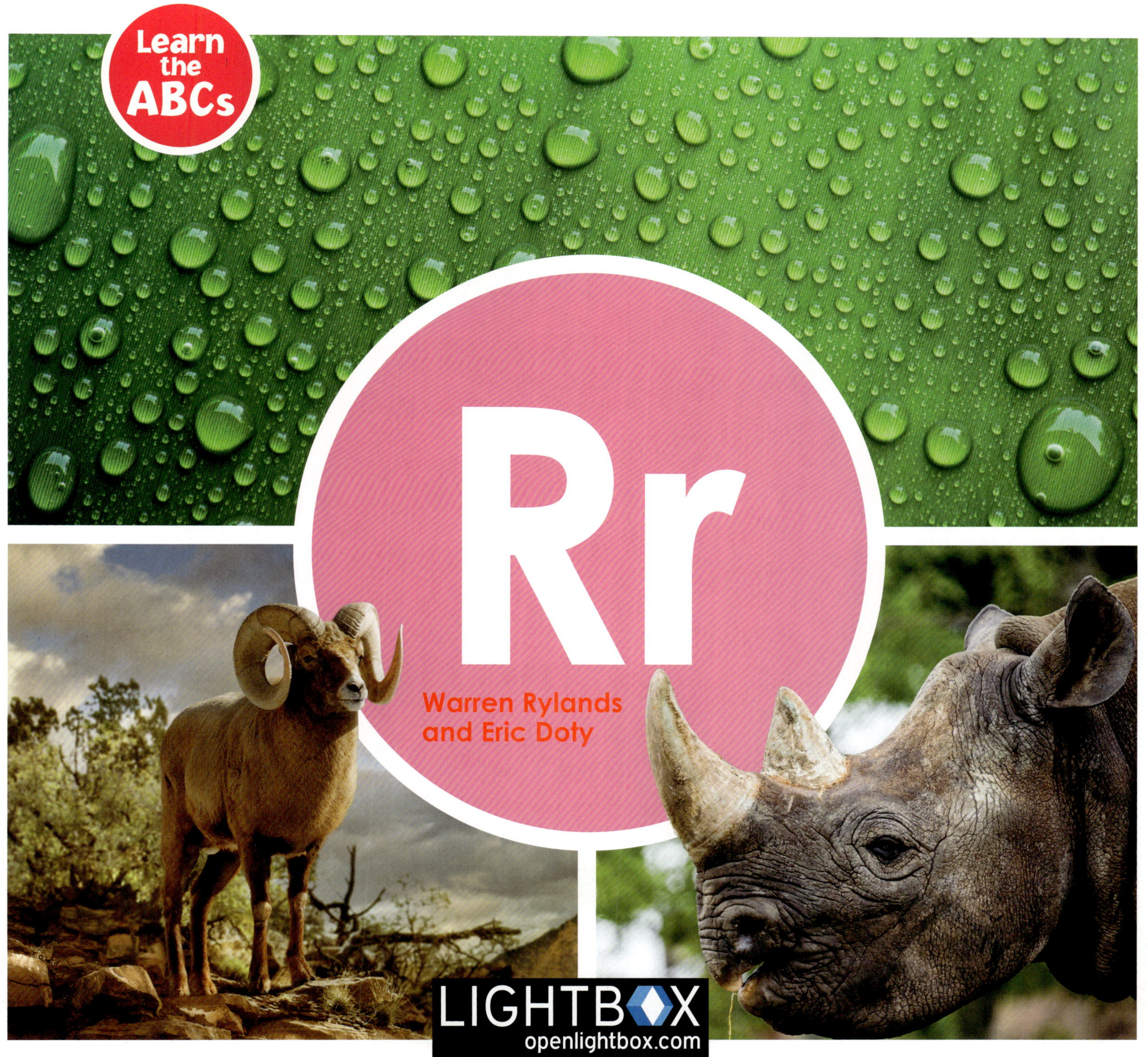
Learn the ABCs
Rr
Warren Rylands
and Eric Doty
LIGHTBOX
openlightbox.com

LIGHTBOX

Go to
www.openlightbox.com
and enter this book's
unique code.

ACCESS CODE

LBXQ2347

Lightbox is an all-inclusive digital solution for the teaching and learning of curriculum topics in an original, groundbreaking way. Lightbox is based on National Curriculum Standards.

OPTIMIZED FOR

- ✓ TABLETS
- ✓ WHITEBOARDS
- ✓ COMPUTERS
- ✓ AND MUCH MORE!

STANDARD FEATURES OF LIGHTBOX

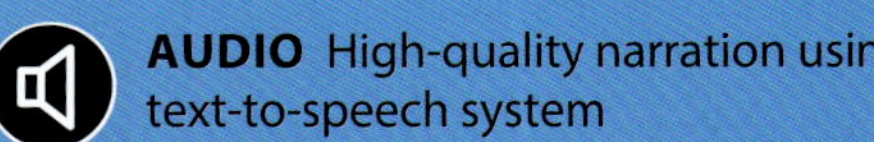
AUDIO High-quality narration using text-to-speech system

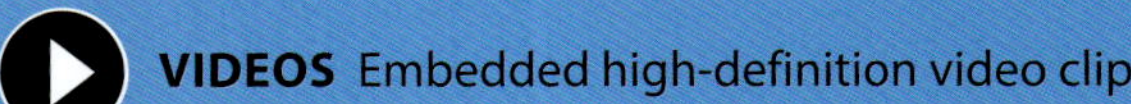
VIDEOS Embedded high-definition video clips

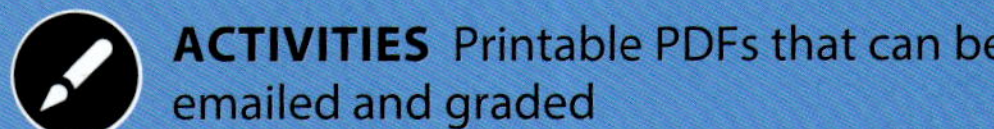
ACTIVITIES Printable PDFs that can be emailed and graded

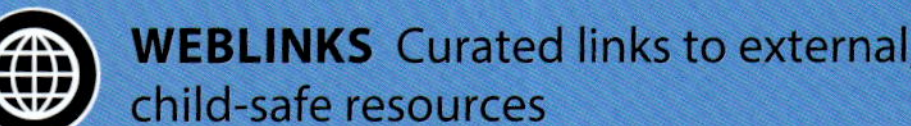
WEBLINKS Curated links to external, child-safe resources

SLIDESHOWS Pictorial overviews of key concepts

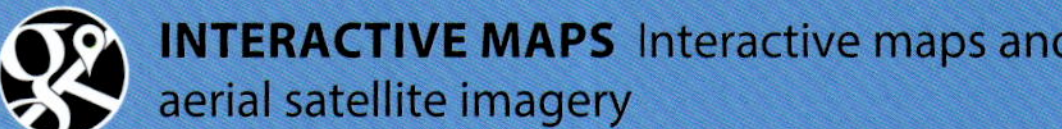
INTERACTIVE MAPS Interactive maps and aerial satellite imagery

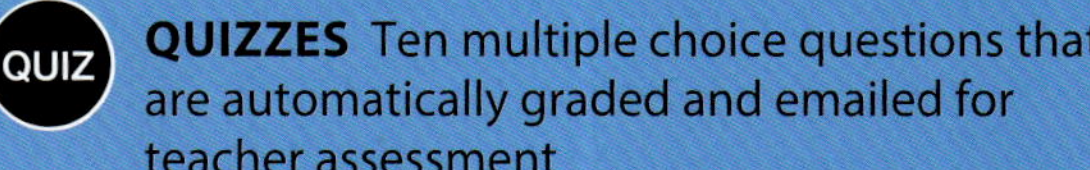
QUIZZES Ten multiple choice questions that are automatically graded and emailed for teacher assessment

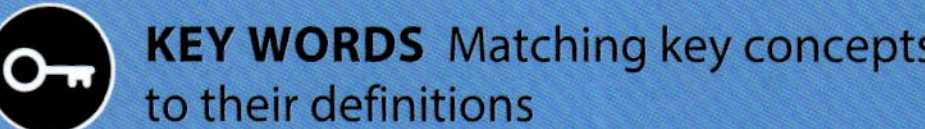
KEY WORDS Matching key concepts to their definitions

VIDEOS

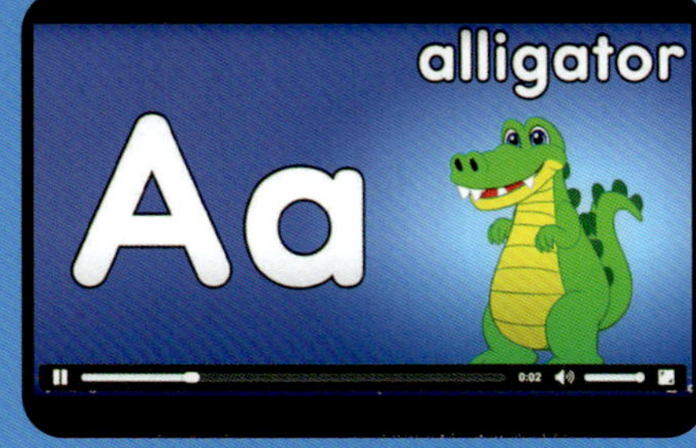

WEBLINKS

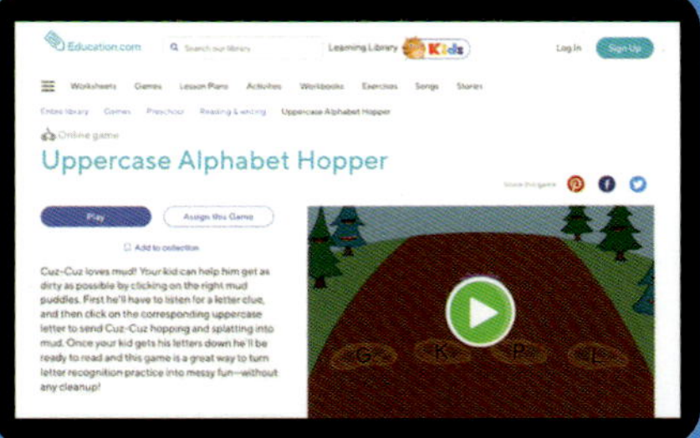

SLIDESHOWS

QUIZZES

This title is part of our Lightbox digital subscription

1-Year K–5 Subscription
ISBN 978-1-5105-5712-3

Access hundreds of Lightbox titles with our digital subscription.
Sign up for a **FREE** subscription trial at **www.openlightbox.com/trial**

Learn the ABCs

Rr

CONTENTS

Let's discover the letter

This is an uppercase R

This is how you write it

This is a lowercase r

This is how you write it

The letter r can start many words.

rhino

rain
robin
run

The letter r can be inside a word.
horse

turtle
yarn
barn
worm

The letter r can be at the end of a word.

bear

four
pear

Many names start with an uppercase R.

Ryan flies a plane.

Raymond plays soccer.

Rose loves plants.

Ron likes burgers.

Ruth has many balloons.

The letter r makes one sound.

berries

rock

The word **rock** has the **r** sound.

The word **berries** also has the **r** sound.

Many words have the r sound.

right
three
around
ever

When the letter r comes twice in a row, it makes only one r sound.

worry
mirror
tomorrow
hurry

Having Fun with R

The rain makes Ruth the rhino worry. Her pears and yard are going to get wet.

Ryan the turtle loves the rain. He runs around and reads in the rain.

Ryan races worms and picks flowers in the rain.

Ruth would rather hide under a rock.

The alphabet has 26 letters.

R is the eighteenth letter in the alphabet.

Aa Bb Cc Dd

Ee Ff Gg Hh Ii Jj

Kk Ll Mm Nn Oo

Pp Qq **Rr** Ss Tt Uu

Vv Ww Xx Yy Zz

KEY WORDS

Research has shown that as much as 65 percent of all written material published in English is made up of 300 words. These 300 words cannot be taught using pictures or learned by sounding them out. They must be recognized by sight. This book contains 48 common sight words to help young readers improve their reading fluency and comprehension. This book also teaches young readers several important content words, such as proper nouns. These words are paired with pictures to aid in learning and improve understanding.

Page	Sight Words First Appearance
4	let, letter, the
5	a, an, how, is, it, this, write, you
6	can, many, start, words
7	run
8	be
10	at, end, of
11	four
12	names, on, with
13	has, likes, plants, plays
14	makes, one, sound
15	also
16	have, read
17	around, right, three
18	comes, in, only, when
20	and, are, get, her, to
21	under, would

Page	Content Words First Appearance
4	Rr
6	ram, rhino
7	rain, robin
8	horse
9	barn, turtle, worm, yarn
10	bear, deer, flower
11	pear
12	Ryan, plane
13	balloons, burgers, Raymond, Ron, Rose, Ruth, soccer
14	berries, rock
18	arrow, row
19	hurry, mirror, tomorrow
20	fun, yard
22	alphabet

Published by Smartbook Media Inc.
276 5th Avenue, Suite 704 #917
New York, NY 10001
Website: www.openlightbox.com

Library of Congress Cataloging-in-Publication Data

Names: Rylands, Warren, author. | Doty, Eric, author.
Title: Rr / Warren Rylands and Eric Doty.
Description: New York, NY : Smartbook Media Inc., [2022] | Series: Learn the ABCs | Audience: Grades K-1
Identifiers: LCCN 2020054178 (print) | LCCN 2020054179 (ebook) | ISBN 9781510557864 (library binding) | ISBN 9781510557888 (ebook other)
Subjects: LCSH: English language--Consonants--Juvenile literature. | English language--Alphabet--Juvenile literature.
Classification: LCC PE1165 .R9539 2022 (print) | LCC PE1165 (ebook) | DDC 421/.1--dc23
LC record available at https://lccn.loc.gov/2020054178
LC ebook record available at https://lccn.loc.gov/2020054179

Printed in Guangzhou, China
1 2 3 4 5 6 7 8 9 0 25 24 23 22 21

022021
110820

Art Director: Terry Paulhus **Project Coordinator:** Sara Cucini

Every reasonable effort has been made to trace ownership and to obtain permission to reprint copyright material. The publisher would be pleased to have any errors or omissions brought to its attention so that they may be corrected in subsequent printings.

The publisher acknowledges Getty Images as the primary image supplier for this title.